I0190713

Timepieces

Yesterday's Stories Today

By Dr. Jeri Fink

Timepieces: Yesterday's Stories Today

By Dr. Jeri Fink

Published by Book Web Publishing, LTD

Book Web Minis

All rights reserved

Copyright 2018

No part of this publication may be reproduced, stored in or introduced into a retrieval system, or transmitted, in any form, or by any means (electronic, mechanical, photocopying, recording, or otherwise), without the prior written permission of the author and/or publisher.

Original and modified cover art by D Sharon Pruitt and CoverDesignStudio.com

ISBN-13: 978-1-941882-29-0

*To Ricky, my husband, friend, and lifelong partner
and our future,
John, Nicky, Mason, and Emma*

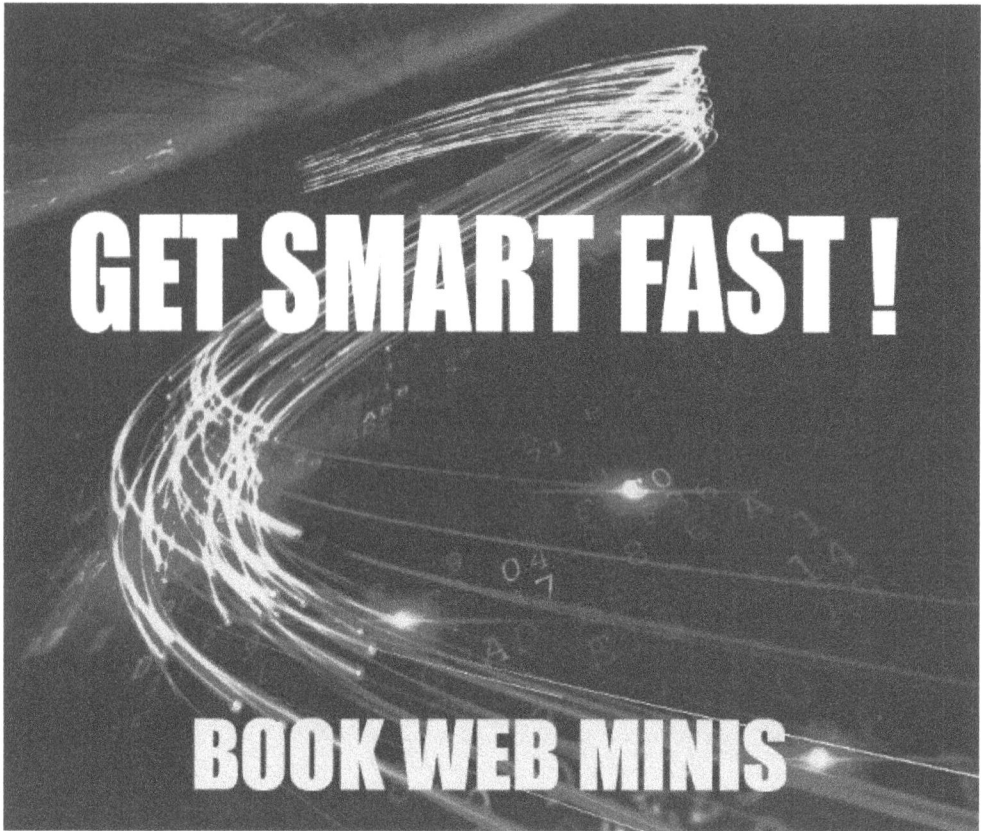

Book Web Minis are fun, fast, and hot. Mini books (50-70 pages) explore up-to-the-minute facts, photos, content, and quizzes to make you the pro. Share with friends, family, and colleagues. Don't wait –in eBook or print from Amazon.com.

Book Web Minis: www.bookwebminis.com

Bestselling Titles:

Paranormal Is My Normal
SOARING
Selfies: Picture Perfect
Timepieces II: Yesterday's Stories Today
Photo Power: Hidden Stories
Pocket Cash: Your Way

Check out Book Web Fiction at
www.hauntedfamilytrees.com
Amazon #1 Bestsellers in print or ebook

Page turners bursting with haunted family trees, strange lovers, chilling photo insights, and psychopaths burst into life. *Broken Books* reinvent the thriller – blending fact, fiction, and photos into riveting stories you'll never forget. Go to amazon.com to purchase these bestsellers in eBook, print (black & white), and collector's edition (full color print).

Contemporary thrillers:

Broken By Truth (Book 1)

Broken By Birth (Book 2)

Broken By Evil (Book 3)

Don't miss Book Web Historical Fiction

Go back in time to discover how good and evil thrived in the past. Meet the ancestors of the characters in the first three *Broken Books* and follow their legacy. Go to amazon.com to purchase these bestsellers in eBook, print (black & white), and collector's edition (full color print).

*Broken By Madness (*Book 4, Dutch New Amsterdam, 1654)

Broken By Men (Book 5, Spain and Portugal, 1490s)

Broken By Kings (Book 6, Sao Tome, Africa, 1494)

Broken: The Prequel (Book 7, Spanish Inquisition, 15th century)

www.hauntedfamilytrees.com

Love photo insights?

Get a FREE image each week in your email that will enlighten, inspire, and make you feel good.

The only requirement is a smile.

Go to: http:// hauntedfamilytrees.com/ landing-page

Timepieces

Yesterday's Stories Today

By Dr. Jeri Fink

with

Dr. Herbert Michelson

Fern Robinson Friedman

Barbara Ryan Woolley

3 Poems by Benjamin Michelson

Why Timepieces? Meet Dr. Jeri Fink

Stories. It's what we're all about.

Today, caught up in the furious pace of our lives, we tell fewer and fewer stories of the past. Our tales are high-tech, political, and global. A slice-of-life from yesterday is often swept beneath expansive stories by professionals – TV and movie people, online storytellers, professional authors, technology dreamers, and others who spin beautiful visual, creative tales.

Timepieces is about true, simple, feel-good stories that give us a glimpse into yesterday. It's filled with photos, fun facts, and real events that would otherwise be forgotten. The stories are about you – your friends, relatives, or acquaintances – who made their worlds richer.

My life is filled with the ordinary and extraordinary; the real and magical. Facts, history, and psychology infuse my imagination. Stories emerge, along with names, photos, and characters. I've written over 30 fiction and nonfiction books, hundreds of blogs and articles, on and offline. I shoot photos, search for abstracted reality, and merge it with words.

The world is my canvas – I've traveled to 6 out of 7 continents, including Antarctica. I've shared my experiences, training, research, and knowledge on television, radio, online, in conferences and workshops, and on prestigious panels like the National Press Club in Washington DC.

As an author, photographer, social worker, and friend, I want to connect with you and the world we share. There's so much to discover.

Visit me on my websites, jerifink.com, hauntedfamilytrees.com, and bookwebminis.com. Discover my fiction on Amazon; read my blogs – especially my favorite, *Whaddya Think, Dr. Fink?* at www.afterfiftylivingliving.com. Check out my feel-good mini books and subscribe to my weekly (free) upbeat photos at hauntedfamilytrees.com/landing-page.

Why Book Web Publishing?

Book Web Publishing produces original mini books in e-book and print formats. If you're interested in doing a mini book check out our website, www.bookwebminis.com and contact me.

Timepieces

Yesterday's Stories Today

Contents

1. *TIKKUN OLAM*

BY DR. JERI FINK

Like Columbus, no one would forget Ben Michelson.

We waited.

Memories filled the cool, moonless night. Images rustled like wind in the trees.

Ben Michelson's story was coming to an end. Like Columbus, no one would forget him.

Ben's life was like a history textbook. He was a first generation New Yorker, the son of Latvian immigrants. English was his native language. He married Rose Liff, a tiny, graceful Eastern European immigrant from Galicia – a territory located between Poland and Ukraine that had once been a part of the Habsburg Austria-Hungary Empire. In 1918 Galicia was annexed by Post-World War One Poland.

Rose arrived in 1902, traveling steerage to New York on the *SS Pennsylvania* owned by the Hamburg America line. Rose was about 16 years old but no one would ever know her exact age. She kept that secret, especially after meeting Ben, who was younger.

Rose and Ben met, eventually got engaged in 1916, and married in 1917. They made a life together when the century was young and the years before them were filled with hope.

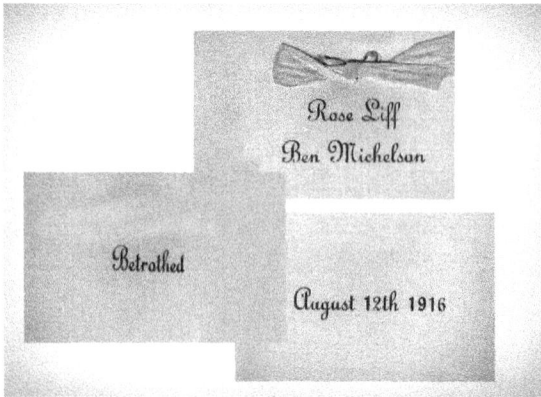

I sat with Rose in the final hours of Ben's life. Rose's eyes fluttered. Perhaps it was the same way when she first met Ben and fell in love? Fifty years had transformed the delicate beauty into a fragile old lady with thin, translucent skin and a soft, sad voice.

Rose and Ben's engagement announcement, 1916

My Grandmother looked at me. "We have to say goodbye."

"Yes," I said softly with all the wisdom a fourteen-year old could muster

Grandma Rose nodded. "He was . . . is . . . a fine man."

I tried to imagine the old face as a young woman without wrinkles, eyes sparkling, in love.

I couldn't.

"You should be proud," she added.

Ben Michelson was a man with a long story, much like the narrative of our people. There was an old belief we embraced, called *tikkun olam*. It meant that each of us had the responsibility to repair, heal, or improve the world.

Ben took it seriously.

As a young man, Ben marched into busy Union Square in New York City, stood on a soapbox, held signs, and gave speeches demanding social justice. He fought for the poor, immigrants, and minorities; his voice was powerful, filled with emotional strength. On Saturdays, Ben would walk down the length of the Bowery. It was a depressing area – the Third Avenue El (elevated subway) ran above the street casting everything in shadows. The area was the city's "Skid Row" with homeless and hopelessly alcoholic men. Ben talked to the men, listened to their stories, and offered help where he could.

"A good man," Rose nodded.

© *Triangle Shirtwaist Factory Fire, 1911*

Grandma Rose also believed deeply in *tikkun olam.* She was a remnant of a past I only knew from books and photos. She left the Triangle Shirt Waist Factory Fire in 1911, two weeks before the deadliest industrial fire in New York City history. 145 sweat shop workers – mostly young women on the upper floors – were burned alive when they couldn't escape through locked or impassable exits. Many of her friends died that day. After the fire, Rose became an active member of the burgeoning International Ladies Garment Workers' Union (ILGWU), fighting sweat shops and exploitation of the poor.

Sometimes I wonder where I would be if she had stayed at the Triangle Waist Factory. Those questions can never be answered.

"Is that why you joined the Ladies Union?" I asked. Rose looked at me strangely. Stories were never about her . . . always Ben.

"Your Grandfather owned a tiny luncheonette," she ignored my question. "He served cab drivers, truckers, and city laborers. One day some dirty cops came." Her voice echoed with pride. "They kicked out his customers and demanded free coffee and food for themselves."

Rose shook her head. "His customers were poor, hard workers. Ben *cared*. He refused to serve the cops. He waited for his regular customers to return. He was the only shopkeeper who had the courage to defy the dirty cops. They shut him down."

I thought of the towering man with the big smile and deep, rough voice who was my Grandfather. He always cared about us *and* others – family, neighbors, and strangers. They said that Ben Michelson had a big heart.

He also loved shiny cars, the horse races, and the fights at Sunnyside Garden Arena in Long Island City. I smile when I remember those stories. Ben spoke about them when he and Rose visited us every Sunday morning, bringing bagels, slabs of lox, salty baked salmon, and rugelach – small pastries filled with everything from apricots and raspberries to chocolate.

"The depression came," Rose continued, "and Ben drove a cab so we could eat."

My Grandfather always made sure his family had food – trading cab rides for leftovers from Mr. Greenburg, a local deli owner, during The Great Depression. When he drove to the "farm" – an abandoned property bought by Great Aunt Anna and Uncle Al – the car was always filled with goodies.

I wondered if I could ever summon that kind of courage. Defy dirty cops? Make a stand for poor people? Speak on a soap box? How much did I believe in *anything*?

"He stuck to what he believed was right."

"I know, Grandma."

Rose looked at me quizzically. *How could I know?* "When Ben could no longer march in Union Square or serve food to city laborers," she continued, "he became one of the first white New Yorkers to join CORE – Congress of Racial Equality – an African-American civil rights organization that started in 1942."

Tikkun Olam. It took a hero to defy the establishment.

Now Ben Michelson was leaving us. He would take his courage and his faith in *Tikkun Olam* with him. He wasn't famous; he didn't write bestseller books or hold political office; and never appeared in a movie, on television, or radio. But we loved him.

"Will the world forget?"

"No," my Grandmother touched my hand as if reading my thoughts. I looked at her wrinkled fingers and swollen, arthritic joints. "No," she said again. "It's like Columbus. Your Grandfather won't be forgotten."

Christopher Columbus? What did Columbus have to do with Ben Michelson?

Rose leaned closer, whispering her secret. "Columbus was Jewish, you know. We've passed that fact down through hundreds of years. He was a Secret Jew hoping to find the Lost Tribe of Israel in the New World."

I would have laughed if my Grandmother hadn't been so serious.

"We all knew The Secret," she continued. "Now you know. A Secret that's over 500 years old."

I was sure that Grandma Rose was silly with grief.

"Just like Columbus," she added, "Ben won't be forgotten."

I pretended to believe her.

A few hours later Ben passed in a tiny, crowded hospital room surrounded by his beloved family. The century moved forward. Years flew by – Grandma Rose passed, then my parents, and two sisters. The new millennium arrived.

I was the last one left.

One day I wandered into a busy New York City bookstore and saw a display about a "new" discovery. There was a sign that proclaimed, "Christopher

Columbus was Jewish."

I froze.

Grandma Rose's voice echoed in my head . . . followed by the whispers of millions that preceded her.

ⓒ *Christopher Columbus*

It's like Columbus. Your Grandfather won't be forgotten.

I bought the books and read each one carefully. New research using old records, letters, and DNA, suggested that Christopher Columbus came from Catalan in Spain. He wasn't Italian like we learned in grade school. Many believed he was from a family of Conversos – Secret Jews who hid their religion and pretended they were converts to Christianity. It was convert or die. They kept their secret in the tunnels and hidden rooms.

Columbus' family fled Catalan and went to Genoa. Columbus' father was a master weaver and for a short time, Christopher worked with him. No one knows why the young man became a sailor.

On his voyage in 1492, Columbus brought along a man named Luis de Torres. He was the official interpreter and one of the few who spoke Hebrew, Aramaic, and Arabic. Torres, also a Secret Jew, was forced to be baptized before sailing with Columbus.

The books said that Columbus expected to find the Lost Tribe of Israel.

I shivered. The past filled me with memories – many inherited and others, like my Grandparents, gleaned from old stories. Suddenly, I understood.

Tikkun Olam was very much alive.

I rushed home to my computer and started to write.

My *Tikkun Olam* is this book. It preserves stories, photos, and details – immortalizing slices of life past. *Timepieces* makes sure Ben Michelson and Rose will not be forgotten.

Near the end of his life, Ben wrote:

Months and years and decades too

All have passed and gone from view.

They trod the road of endless time

And left their mark on you.

Timepieces drift through the years, embedded in stories we hear, tell, and share.

Ben Michelson, 1930

Time Pix

Rose, Ben, and their first granddaughter, Sandra

Rose, 1917

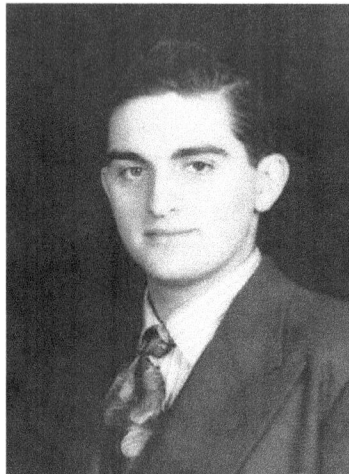

Son Herbert, 1944

Daughter Ruth, 1940 (my mother)

The Bowery, New York City, 1938

Library of Congress #USZ62-93-754

Facts about *Tikkun Olam*

*Former President Barack Obama declared in 2010, at the first White House Reception for Jewish American Heritage Month, that America must "uphold the principle of Tikkun Olam – our obligation to repair the world."

*Each year, Hadassah gives the Australia Tikkun Olam Award to the Australian who "demonstrates the finest qualities and traditions of medicine, sciences, teaching, and humanity."

*Tikkun Olam Makers (TOM) is a global movement made up of communities that connect designers, developers, and engineers to people with disabilities for the purpose of developing technological solutions for daily challenges.

**Tikkun* is a Jewish magazine with the tagline, "to heal, repair, and transform the world."

*Many people associate the phrase Tikkun Olam with social justice and action.

*The Tikkun Olam Women's Foundation of Greater Washington offers grants to organizations that work to help women and girls in their community and Israel.

*Beth Shalom Synagogue of Wake County, North Carolina, writes on their home page, "We dedicate ourselves to . . . Tikkun Olam – repairing the world – through acts of kindness, social justice, loving our neighbor, and caring for God's creation."

*Diller Tikkun Olam awards $36,000 to each of 15 Jewish U.S. Teens for "exceptional leadership and engagement in service projects to make the world a better place."

*Tikkun Olam Tel Aviv-Jaffa is a post-college internship to start young people in careers with non-profit organizations.

*There are blogs, websites, social movements, magazines, organizations, and books with Tikkun Olam in their titles and philosophy.

*The Israel Forum for International Humanitarian Aid (IsraAid) is a humanitarian organization that helps in disaster relief, search and rescue, medical assistance micro-financing, and psychotraumatic care for people and countries around the world. It is made up of over 35 humanitarian aid organizations, youth movements, solidarity movements, and friendship societies reflecting the soul of Tikkun Olam.

Popular expressions that describe Tikkun Olam:

Making the world a better place

Repairing the World

Acting justly toward people in need

Healing the world

Mending the world

Three Poems by Ben Michelson (1896-1961)

WAR ∗∗∗∗∗∗∗∗∗∗∗∗∗ NO MORE

When the roar of the battle has ended

And the strife of the conflicts' no more,

When the Victor and Vanquished have blended

We MUST---- at all cost ----- Banish WAR!

When the Peace has been made and attested

With all Nations united as one,

When a would-be aggressor's ARESTED

Then we'll know that with WAR we are done!

So, let's look for the coming of REASON

To a world soaked in blood and despair

As the farmer awaits every season

While we wait ---- let us work ---- and PREPARE!

You're old, too old, too old!

Months and years and decades too

All have passed and gone from view

They trod the road of endless time

And left their mark on you.

A knob that's turned, a button pressed

An unseen hand writes on!

An iron bird flies overhead

Now there, now here, now gone!

A picture clear from far and near

Comes through the air to you

You wonder how, to ask you fear,

The answer known to but a few.

What means this life we hang on to

What is there left to say . . . to do?

What story still untold?

What wonders to unfold?

What will the future bring to us

Upon a distant morn

What goal to seek . . . what aim to reach

What miracles unborn?

Will we attain those visioned dreams?

To see and hear and hold

Or will we leave them all and hear

"You're old, too old, too old!"

Mountains, and forests, and streams

Mountains and forests and streams

Wonderful topics of dreams

Where nature displays, in myriad ways,

Her fabulous, breath-taking themes.

In science we find, many men with a mind

To discover or build something new

But where can you find, yes where can you see

A man who can build you a tree?

The artist, the sculptor, the architect too,

Might build you from metal a fountain

But not among these though you seek the world through

Will you find one to build a real mountain!

Fishermen, sailors, mariners all

Afloat on the water, in craft large and small,

Secure in the safety of radio's beam

Can any of these build a stream?

The sages, the wise men, dreamers of dreams,

Have left us our heritage, reams upon reams

But where can you find, in all of their themes,

How to build mountains, and forests, and streams?

2. *FIND THE JEROBONGAS!*

DR. HERBERT MICHELSON

War! The Kelly Street Boys crept into our territory. We grabbed guns made from fruit-crate ends and bullets cut out of shirt cardboard from the hand laundry.

757 Beck Street Today

It was the early 1930s. I lived at 757 Beck Street in East Bronx, New York. The block was relatively quiet unless we were in battle playing war, ring-a-levio or world class stickball in the street. Many family members lived in our building or further down the block. There were aunts, uncles, cousins - no one was very far away until we declared a cease fire, climbed into Pop's car, and headed north to the "farm."

Pop loved his car. We all did. He drove a Model A Ford with velvet seats and tassels on the rear window.

He piled in Mother, my older sister Ruth, me, and Patsy, our beloved Boston Bull Terrier. Then came the clothes, bedding, and food.

We were off.

In those days, Pop worked as a taxi driver. He had made a deal with Mr. Greenberg, the deli owner: taxi rides for food. Mr. Greenberg was driven for free all over the Bronx; in turn, we ate salami, pastrami, and other leftover deli goodies from his store.

Pop always made sure we had enough food before he drove back to the city. He never stayed at the farm.

"I'm a city boy," he explained, "no country for me."

The farm wasn't a real working operation with horses, cows, and crops. Aunt Anna and Uncle Al had had bought the abandoned property for next to nothing after the Great Depression hit.

There were over 60 acres, including an ancient apple orchard, lots of berry bushes, an old farmhouse, crumbling barn, and a chicken coop with a sloped roof. The farmhouse was so small that the family took turns visiting. The boys slept on the floor in the unfinished attic; the girls and women were downstairs in a room connected by a stovepipe to the attic.

The closest neighbor was the tiny Medler dairy farm – it took an hour of downhill walking to get there. We bought milk and of a piece of Mrs. Medler's mouthwatering walnut cake. When Mr. Medler milked the cow, he let us city kids watch. If he was in a good mood and we were standing too close, he would spray the milk right into our faces!

My cousin Danny was my best friend. Together we braved the dark creatures that lived in the woods and hunted mythical critters like the *albatrich*. Someone had created the evil albatrich, but as hard as we tried, we never found one. Danny and

Ruth and Buddy at the farm

I held jumping competitions off the chicken coop roof and walked the plank on the high creaky beams in the barn – always keeping a wary eye for monsters who lurked in the shadows and the rattlesnakes we were told lived there - even though we never heard or saw them.

When things were quiet, we made up pranks. Sometimes Ruth joined us and other times she was the target. She was eight years older than me and that meant a lot in those days.

One of our favorite pranks was when we told the girls there were dangerous rattlesnakes loose in the basement.

Danny, Buddy (Danny's older brother), and I spent days embellishing the story. The girls were so scared that no one noticed when we threaded a wire through the stovepipe to their beds. We attached the wire to the metal bedframes and ran upstairs to wait. When the girls fell asleep we connected the wire to a vibrating coil lifted from an old Model T Ford rotting in the hayfield. Then we hit it – sending an electric shock and buzzing sound down the wire. The girls leaped out of their beds, convinced the rattlesnakes were attacking. We supported their imagination and bravely "cleared" their beds while secretly reattaching the wires.

We laughed as hard as the girls screamed.

At night, when the gasoline lamp was turned on, we thought of new games. The frayed monopoly game that lived in the kitchen got boring. That's when we came up with our favorite, *Find the Jerobongas Tree!* We invented the name and claimed it was magical – a good luck charm. Jeronbongas trees were always surrounded by the sweetest blackberry and raspberry bushes I've ever tasted. It was actually a large Maple that turned golden yellow as autumn approached. But who cared about facts? The "finder" got to wear a floppy straw hat for the day.

The game began with a shout, *"Find the Jerobongas!"* Every kid raced into the woods. We filled silver metal buckets with berries and rushed home, our lips purple from the juice. The women transformed our harvest into sweet jam that we ate through the winter.

One hot summer day Ruth called out loud and clear. "I found the *Jerobongas* Tree!"

We rushed to her. Ruth had won! She received the winner's right to wear the prized straw hat for the day while we were rewarded with fistfuls of berries.

Eventually, everyone left with their buckets. Danny and I lingered, reluctant to head home. We sat by the Jerobongas, our backs against a rocky outcrop leftover from an abandoned quarry, and watched the sunset. We waited for the stars to come out. There were so many of them – so different from our city sky.

Something lingered in the air – a suggestion of impending history.

"What do you think is going to happen when we grow up?" Danny asked softly.

"Maybe we'll be famous?"

"Maybe we'll be rich?"

"Maybe," I sighed, "we'll have a whole farm of *Jerobongas*."

We laughed and stared at the dark sky. Our lives and the entire universe lay before us.

Night sounds emerged – an animal skittering through the woods, an owl hooting, wind rustling through leaves. It was the kind of peace we could only find with a *Jerobongas Tree*.

We were quiet for a very long time.

"We'll be OK," Danny said finally.

"Yeah," I agreed, "as long as the Jerobongas is with us."

We laughed roguishly, knowing our mothers would scold us for being out so late. Finally we stood, shook hands in a very manly way, and ran back to the tiny, crowded farmhouse.

Years later, when the world was fighting a war that would eventually kill over 60 million people, we went to battle. This time we didn't carry fruit-crate guns and cardboard bullets. Danny joined the Navy and Buddy went into the Army, both fighting Nazis in Europe. I enlisted and became an Army medic. I was sent to the South Pacific.

In 1945 I was shipped out of Guam as part of the occupying force in Korea. I was in a large convoy of troop carriers and destroyers. We were transported across the China Sea in the *USS Rotanin*. A typhoon hit, along with an undersea earthquake. The waves and wind were massive - we bounced around like a roller coaster.

I was in a bottom bunk. Each guy hung his helmet at the head of his bunk for seasickness. Others were lashed to the deck, too nauseous to stay below. Some lay with their heads in the salt water showers. There were ropes everywhere so we could move from place to place. The destroyers that escorted us flew the American flag from their sterns. That was the nicest thing I could see.

USS Rotanin

I thought I was going to die.

Suddenly the magical words echoed in my mind, louder than the maelstrom outside.

Find the Jerobongas!

I saw the farm, Danny, Buddy, and Ruth. We were racing through the woods.

Find the Jerobongas and we'll be OK.

We were in different parts of the world but I knew they were feeling the same magic. I smiled. The *Jerobongas* was with us.

We all survived the war.

Over eighty years have passed and I still vividly recall those times. I remember my youth, the war, and the beloved farm. I'm 92 years old now. I hope that my children and grandchildren carry the magic of the *Jerobongas* deep inside them.

I dream of a world that's not too busy, self-serving, or techy for such things.

Time pix

"The *experience* of time is different for us all . . . we alter our perception of time, nothing more, by ordinary means." – Herbert J. Michelson, Ph.D, *Consciousness: The infinite journey*, 2004.

My sister Ruth, at the farm, 1933

The Michelson family: Pop (Ben), Mother (Rose), me, Ruth, 1935

My son, Kevin, 2009

Me in uniform, 1944

My grandkids, Jason & Sam

Me today

Facts from the 1930s

A soup kitchen line during the Great Depression

Courtesy of The Library of Congress – New York World-Telegram & Sun Collection

*The Great Depression began after the 1929 Stock Market Crash and ended in 1939 with World War 2

*About 6000 people sold apples on the streets in New York City, hoping to avoid the shame of panhandling.

*Zippers were widely used because buttons were too expensive.

*The biggest hit song (1932) was Bing Crosby's *Brother, Can You Spare a Dime?*

*Herbert Hoover took office in 1929 – at the beginning of the Great Depression. People who lost their homes often lived in *Hoovervilles* or shanty towns; *Hoover Stew* was dished out in soup kitchens; newspapers used as blankets were called *Hoover Blankets;* jackrabbits used for food were *Hoover Hogs;* and broken cars pulled by mules were *Hoover Wagons.*

*The Empire State building, Chrysler building, Golden Gate Bridge, and Rockefeller Center were all built from Great Depression worker relief programs.

*At the peak of the great depression 25% of the population was out of work.

*Scotch tape was invented by Richard Drew as a cheap way to make things last.

*President Hoover announced in March 1930 that the U.S. had "passed the worst."

*During the Great Depression, 60 to 80 million people went to the movies each week. It was a low-cost way to escape from the reality of poverty and unemployment. The average ticket was 25 cents.

*Banks were hated because so many failed. Bank robbers like Bonnie and Clyde became American folk heroes.

*Radio thrived. It was cheap or free and there were variety shows, news, and music. One of the favorites was a serial show, *Amos 'n Andy* – over forty million people listened. The show was set in Harlem, Manhattan's well-known Afro-American community. Below left, Freeman Gosden (left – the voice of Amos and Kingfish) and Charles Correll (the voice of Andy) celebrated the 10th anniversary of the radio program on March 18, 1938. Next to it on the right is a 1930 drawing of the "real" characters.

Wikimedia Commons

36

3. *IT HAPPENED IN '59*

BY FERN ROBINSON FRIEDMAN

It was the worst (and best) day of my life.

I was ten years old. Mr. Dundon's fifth grade class was buzzing with excitement. PS 213 was a fairly new school – the classroom had a wall of windows on one side and on the other side, closets with folding doors. Inside the closets we hung coats and stored lunchboxes. The classroom was filled with wood school desks placed in long even rows.

Mr. Dundon, wearing a blue tie and dress pants smiled at the class. He was one of the most popular teachers in the school. He introduced me to the class as the new kid. No one cared. It was Valentine's Day.

The sea of strange faces and names ignored me. I shivered.

In 1959 New York City public schools, Valentine's Day was a big deal. Everyone brought books of punch-out cards to school. They were small colorful cards with pictures of happy kids, stuffed animals, and puppies. You selected a card, punched it out, and then wrote who would get it and your name. The best cards had a touch of flock around the edges.

When the teacher said it was time, all the kids raced around the classroom delivering cards to their friends. It was crazy with laughing, teasing, and noisy kids.

The most popular kids had a big pile of cards on their desks. The least popular had the smallest pile. Everyone got at least one card.

Except me.

Voices rose in the classroom.

Does Jimmy have a crush on Susan?

Does Valerie have more cards than Charlie?

A voice rang out. *Bobby and Audrey sitting in a tree . . . ki. . . ss. . .ing.*

Mr. Dundon's class was having a great time.

I hung my head and fought the tears. My parents didn't get it. Why would they move on Valentine's Day? There was only one answer: to make me miserable.

We had lived in a court in Springfield Gardens Apartments. They were small, cheap apartments in Bayside, Queens, New York. The buildings were old. My sister and I shared a tiny bedroom and the gas stove in the kitchen had only one burner. My dad caught the Q75 bus at the corner to go to work. He was a civil engineer who helped design one of Robert Moses' pet project – the Meadowbrook Parkway. Moses was known for building parkways that went straight through settled neighborhoods. Nearby our home, there was an entire community of private houses that had been moved, on-by-one, to a golf course off Horace Harding Boulevard. That's how The Clearview Expressway was born.

The owners complained but no one cared - like the kids in Mr. Dundon's class.

Mom shook her head and grumbled, "Robert Moses always gets his way."

I didn't know what she meant but I sure knew about moving. All my friends lived in the court and here I was, alone, in a new class, with everyone around me having fun. I dreamed about playing potsy on a chalk board on the street or punch ball where the bases were garbage cans.

I knew those days were over.

In our new house on Cloverdale Boulevard I had my own room but no friends. I stared at the scratches and doodles carved into my wood school desk and tried to pretend that I was somewhere else.

Suddenly a single card was put on my desk. I couldn't believe my eyes. I looked up at a girl with warm brown eyes and frizzy black hair.

"Happy Valentine's Day," she said softly. "What's your name?"

"Fern," I said shyly. "My name is Fern."

It's funny how a small act of kindness can last a lifetime.

Jeri lived a few blocks away on 228th Street on the other side of Cloverdale Boulevard. She also had her own room. Even better was the hill in the front. We used to roll up and down the hill, inventing all kinds of games. Those days it looked like the biggest hill in the world. This is how Jeri's house looks today.

Sometimes we hung around inside, drinking "seltzer." Today it's called club soda but in 1959 it was brought to the house. A dirty wood crate with dividers was

filled with heavy, thick-glass seltzer bottles delivered weekly by the "seltzer man" – a short, fat guy with a cigar dangling from his mouth. He smelled awful. We held our noses and giggled when he passed by.

These days a "vintage seltzer bottle" sells for over $100. Who knew?

Jeri and I spent hours talking about boys, comparing notes on who was popular, who was cute, and later, why we hated math at Junior High School PS74.

Sometimes we poured thick *U-bet* Chocolate Syrup into a glass, mixed it with milk, and added seltzer. It bubbled up into what was called an "egg cream." There was no eggs or cream in it but lots of theories about the name. We later found out that some people believe it was invented by Eastern European Jewish immigrants in the 1880s. Others claim that it was pure New York – as native as me and Jeri.

These days we try to imitate it with chocolate syrup, 2% milk, and club soda. It doesn't taste the same.

As the 1959 school year came to a close, we headed for sixth grade.

Jimmy and Susan broke up. Popular Valerie became a snob and no one liked her. Bobby and Audrey were found making out in the woods behind the school – a place called Alley Pond Park. Everyone called her a slut until she moved away in 7th grade.

Jeri and I went to Junior High School together in a special program called the SPs. We had to pass the test to be in the program. Kids in the SPs did 7th, 8th, and 9th grades in two years, making us one year ahead of the non-SP kids.

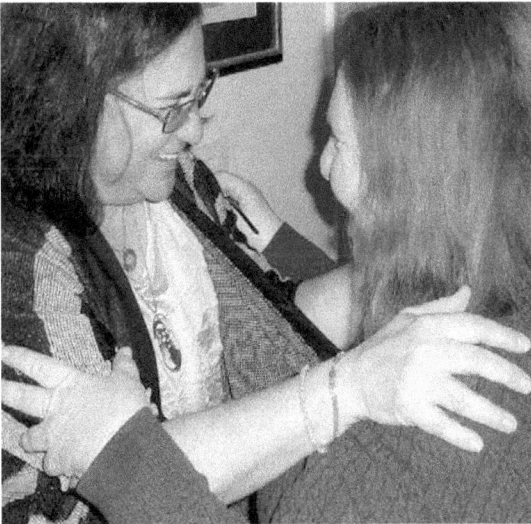

At the end of ninth grade Jeri moved away to Long Island. We still talked every day. An hour drive couldn't stop us.

Jeri and I have been best friends now for almost 60 years.

I was married in 1969 and Jeri was married in 1970. We were bridesmaids in each other's weddings. I found their first apartment in the same building where I lived. A few years later my husband and I moved to California.

We raised our families "together" 3000 miles apart in Los Angeles and New York. We visited, ran up phone bills, went to email, and now text. It didn't change our friendship.

Our lives were permanently connected that day in 1959.

We still talk almost every day, visit each other, and when we get the chance, take trips together. We've explored places like Sedona, Arizona, Sequoia National Park in California, Las Vegas, and Manhattan. Our birthdays are 3 weeks apart so we celebrated "our" 60th in London.

These days I'm a realtor in Los Angeles. I live with my husband and daughter Melissa and spend a lot of time with my grandchildren, Laila and Andrew.

Now I'm telling our story in Jeri's book – a very special timepiece. We've shared a lifetime.

All because of a punch-out Valentine's card and a little girl who cared.

Time pix

Me (left), Jeri (standing), NY friends Donna and Cindy

Me Shopping at Macy's in New York

My family at my daughter Rachel's wedding

Celebrating our 60th birthdays in London

My grandchildren, Andrew and Laila

Fun facts from 1959

*The Barbie doll was launched.

*Alaska became the 49th state of the United States.

*_Bonanza_ premiered on NBC – the first weekly TV series broadcast completely in color. Other popular TV westerns were _Gunsmoke_, _Wagon Train_, and _Have Gun Will Travel_ – James Arness (left) played Matt Dillon on _Gunsmoke_.

*The first episode of _Twilight Zone_ aired.

*The chartered plane flying Buddy Holly, Richie Valens, and the Big Bopper Jiles Richardson) went down in an Iowa snowstorm. No one survived. The tragedy was later popularized by Don McClean's song, _The Day the Music Died._

*Elvis Presley, Doris Day, Frank Sinatra, and Ella Fitzgerald were a few of the most popular singers.

*_Xerox_ launched the first commercial copy machine.

*Fidel Castro assumed power in Cuba.

*The second annual Grammy awards gave _Mack the Knife_ (Bobby Darin, right) the "Record of The Year."

*Glen Raven Mills introduced panty hose, designed by Allen Gant in 1953 and called "panti legs."

*_Ben-Hur_ was the highest grossing movie, winning 11 Oscars.

*_Big Hunk of Love_ by Elvis Presley was a hit.

*Gasoline cost 25 cents a gallon.

*_Bozo the Clown_ premiered on TV.

*_Time Magazine's_ "Man of the Year" was Dwight D. Eisenhower.

*Marilyn Monroe and Tony Curtis (right) starred in the movie, _Some Like It Hot_.

*_Playboy_ magazine debuted with Marilyn Monroe as the centerfold.

*The most popular baby names were Mary and Michael.

*_Gigi_ won the Oscar for best film

*The average cost of a new house was $12,400.

*The average yearly wage was $5,010.

*A movie ticket cost $1.

*Soviet Premier Nikita Khrushchev was denied his request to visit Disneyland.

*Some of the most popular female stars were Elizabeth Taylor, Brigitte Bardot, Sophia Loren, Donna Reed, and Audrey Hepburn.

*It was rumored that Rock Hudson and Doris Day were a couple. In 1985 Rock Hudson revealed he was gay and had AIDS.

*George Reeves, the original Superman, died from a gunshot wound at the age of 45. Police ruled his death a suicide but there were rumors he was murdered. No arrests or convictions were made.

*Doris Day (left) and Rock Hudson stared in the movie *Pillow Talk.*

*Neil Sedaka had his first international hit with the song, *Oh! Carol.* It was for his high school girlfriend, Carol Klein – who later achieved success as Carole King.

*The *rat pack* first appeared – Frank Sinatra, Dean Martin, Sammy Davis Jr., Peter Lawford, and Joey Bishop.

*The original troll doll was created by a Danish woodworker, Thomas Dam, as a gift for his daughter.

*The most popular Christmas gifts was a *Barbie* doll and the game of *Risk.*

Tang drink mix was introduced in powdered form.

*Hawaii became the 50th state of the United States.

*NASA introduced the *Mercury Seven* (below) – the original Astronauts who made space history. They were: (front row left to right) Walter Schirra, Donald Slayton, John Glenn, Scott Carpenter; (back row), Alan Shepard, Gus Grissom, and Gordon Cooper.

4. *AUNTIE*

BY BARBARA RYAN WOOLLEY

The year was 1932.

Fifteen cents bought you a thick, juicy hamburger and coffee. A full lunch, including pie, cost twenty-five cents. There were three busy spigots – for syrup, soda, and beer.

It was The Great Depression and the Eisenstein family had done the impossible.

Businesses were closing everywhere – the economy was shattered. Using all the money he had in the world, 23-year old Sam Eisenstein opened a newsstand-soda fountain and named it *Sam's*. It was on Gedney Way, a dirt road far from the White Plains, NY business district and near the Westchester-Boston Railroad Station.

"It will never make it," the locals said.

Sam proved otherwise. He was always busy. There were commuters coming off the train and "commuters" who told their wives they were going to work and when the coast was clear, went to *Sam's* instead. They laughed while drinking 35-cent shots of whiskey and 10-cent beers.

Sam's sister Dora (Auntie) joined the business. She was 16 years old. Brother Joe signed on. Sam's became one of the most popular watering holes in town, filling the restaurant with good food, music, and comradery. Whether families, coaches, teams, road workers, or just regular locals, they all had a great time.

Sam's and Auntie were part of my family for as long as I can remember.

Everyone loved Sam (left), "Auntie" Dora, and Joe. Auntie was full of life and laughter, playing with the kids, chatting with the adults, and listening to family stories. She never forgot a name or story. Auntie knew everyone and everyone knew her.

White Plains loved the Eisenstein family. Sam was "elected" the "Mayor of Gedney Way" which became a tagline for the restaurant. The city honored Auntie by putting a street sign on the corner of the restaurant parking lot. Sam's was – and still is – one of the most popular spots in town.

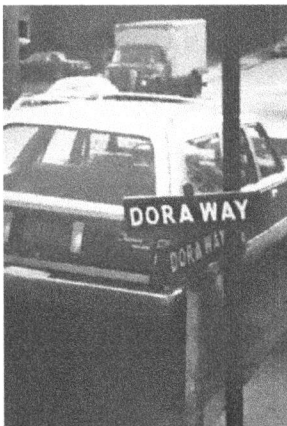

Auntie was well known for checking up on the diners – going from table to table to make sure everyone was having a good time. She marveled over growing kids, asked after ailing relatives, and listened to heartwarming stories. The locals were just as important as the celebrities. At the same time, Auntie was deeply involved with our family, remembering every detail, always wanting to know how

I was doing, and never missing a dinner or event.

"She was a beautiful spirit," Stacy Brown wrote in *The Journal News*.

Sam's rocked with sports figures, politicians, barbershop singers, business people, reporters, media types, and anyone who wanted to join the fun. People like Judge William Blakely, the first Westchester County Executive, Gene Rayburn (TV host of *Match Game*), Lou Gehrig, and Rita Hayworth showed up, laughing next to coaches, salesmen, and other locals. Many of the gentlemen flirted with Auntie. She always responded with a smile, "If it's on the menu you can have it. If it's not on the menu you can't."

In those days, the place had dark wood paneled walls, wood floors, and booths with red seats and wood backs. The long, eye-catching wood bar was backed with mirrors and glass shelves holding colorful liquor bottles. The round red leather bar seats twirled around in a full circle so customers could have conversations with folks in all directions.

What fun I had playing on those stools!

Sam's was both elegant and comfortable – a place for families and kids, romantic dates, and sports people from athletes and announcers to coaches. Almost every night there was a piano player, crooning favorites like *My Blue Heaven* and *My Buddy*.

One night during the 1930s, a baseball player, along with his entourage, arrived at Sam's. Twelve big men huddled around tables pushed together. They ordered steaks, Sam's celebrated onion rings, French fries, and salad with the restaurant's legendary blue cheese dressing. Beer and whiskey flowed.

"They ran me ragged," Auntie recalled.

As usual, Auntie checked the table throughout the night, making sure everyone was having a good time. Suddenly one of the "gentlemen" tapped her knee. Auntie assumed he was being "fresh."

She ignored him.

He tapped her knee again, refusing to give up.

She finally looked at him. The gentleman was the most famous baseball player of the time - Babe Ruth!

The Babe was known for his unrivaled athletic skills along with his love of parties and women. Sometimes called "The Great Bambino," Babe had a candy named after him – a chocolate covered bar filled with peanuts, caramel, and nougat called Baby Ruth. Eventually, Baby Ruth became "the official candy bar of major league baseball" and the first candy bar to profit from a celebrity name.

The Babe smiled boyishly at Auntie. His grin was charming. He knew just what she was thinking – no one could resist The Babe.

"I was just trying to thank you for your great food and service," he said innocently as he handed her a $20 tip. Twenty dollars in those days is equivalent to $400 dollars today!

Auntie accepted the tip and the two of them laughed. It was a sweet moment that she would remember for the rest of her life.

Auntie never married but she adored her family and treated her nieces and nephews like her own children. Everyone loved her.

She was my Godmother (along with my older brother Ricky). She watched us grow up to become parents, embracing the new members in our family. Thousands of other kids passed through Sam's as well, often working as waiters and waitresses. Her other nieces and nephews worked there, bringing friends and making memories. The day her my brother Ricky got engaged he drove to Sam's with his fiancé so Auntie would be the first in the family to know!

Sometimes it's the small things that you remember so well. I was in high school and worked at Sam's during my school breaks. One summer I noticed that my mom needed a new vacuum cleaner. I saved all my salary and tips from Sam's and told Auntie I wanted to buy Mom the vacuum cleaner as a surprise.

Auntie immediately went into action. She called one of her friends who was a vacuum cleaner salesman to meet me at Sam's. He advised me what to get and gave me a great deal. His selection, though, was out of my budget. Auntie stepped in with the extra money I needed. To this day I remember the surprise and pleasure on Mom's face (and Auntie's) when I gave her the vacuum.

These days I think about when I sat at the bar while Auntie brought me a huge plate of onion rings and a hot roast beef sandwich on an onion garlic roll with her homemade dressing. I recall swirling around on the bar stools, Auntie laughing with pleasure. I can taste the food and feel the love.

Auntie is long gone now but Sam's still thrives on Gedney Way. You can go inside and see all the old photos and have a delicious meal – although it will cost you more than 15 cents!

Today's owners, Peter and Karen Herrero, both natives of White Plains, welcome everyone warmly with the same spirit of the original Sam's, "incorporating the best of then with the best of now."

I have brought my husband and family to Sam's, telling them stories from the old days. They look at the photos – still on the wall – and see what it was like. My brother comes with his kids and grandkids, too.

Auntie still lives in the warmth of Sam's and the hearts of all of us who loved her.

My brother Ricky in front of Sam's wall of old photos

Time Pix

Tavern on the Green, 1967

(left to right) Edna (Auntie's sister and my mom), brother-in-law Harvey (my dad), Auntie, me and my brother Ricky

My family today

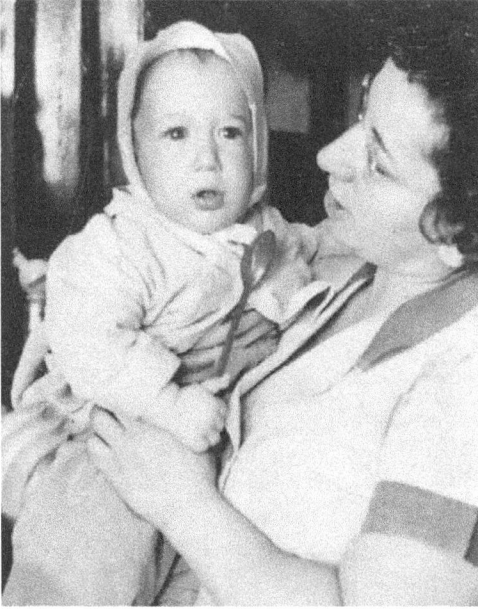

Auntie and Ricky, 1949

Ricky's family, Father's Day at Sam's

Laughing with Auntie (left: Jeri, Edna, Auntie, Ricky, me) 1971

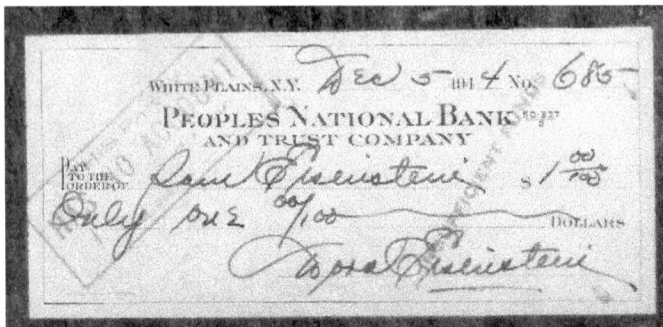

Money was tight in 1944 – a returned check for $1

Fun Facts About Sam's and White Plains

*Sam's received one of the first three liquor licenses granted in Westchester County after Prohibition was repealed in 1933.

*Sam's was the first New York State bar to put in a TV.

*Today, Sam's donates two percent of its annual sales to organizations like the Food Bank for Westchester and Scarsdale-Edgemont Family Services Organization.

*The last train to White Plains on the Westchester & Boston line was on December 31, 1937.

*Mark Zuckerberg, founder of Face Book was born in White Plains, May 14, 1984.

*White Plains was first settled in 1683 when a group of men purchased 4,435 acres of land from the Weckquaeskeck Indians.

*George Washington and his troops fought the Battle of White Plains on October 28, 1776. They were forced to retreat but stopped the British campaign.

*Auntie spent her entire life in the house on 35 Cleveland Street, White Plains.

*Puritans from Connecticut settled in White Plains in the 1600s.

*White Plains is 25 miles northeast of midtown New York.

*Ralph Waite, the actor, was born in White Plains on June 22, 1928.

*After Sam and Joe passed away, Auntie sold Sam's in 1980. She volunteered at White Plains Hospital. She received the hospital's Volunteerism award in 1997 for her work at the hospital and her commitment to the American Cancer Society and the American Heart Association.

*56,853 people live in White Plains today.

*Actor James Whitmore was born in 1921 in White Plains.

*White Plains is the county seat of Westchester County, NY – one of the most expensive counties in the country.

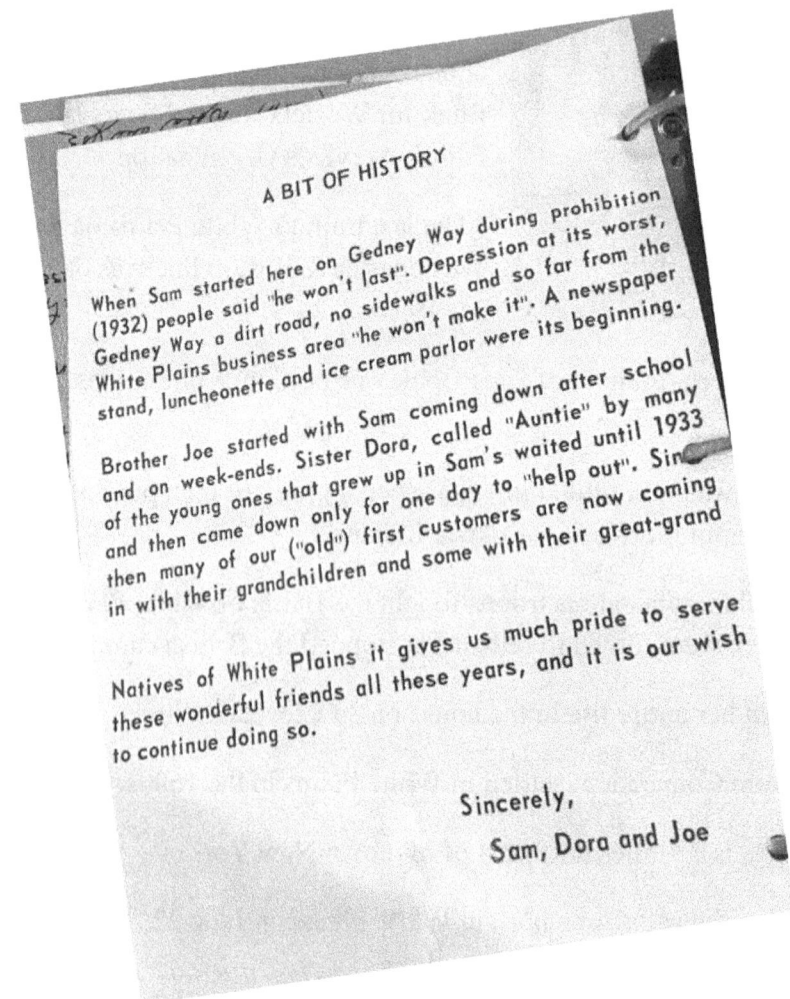

A BIT OF HISTORY

When Sam started here on Gedney Way during prohibition (1932) people said "he won't last". Depression at its worst, Gedney Way a dirt road, no sidewalks and so far from the White Plains business area "he won't make it". A newspaper stand, luncheonette and ice cream parlor were its beginning.

Brother Joe started with Sam coming down after school and on week-ends. Sister Dora, called "Auntie" by many of the young ones that grew up in Sam's waited until 1933 and then came down only for one day to "help out". Sin[ce] then many of our ("old") first customers are now coming in with their grandchildren and some with their great-grand

Natives of White Plains it gives us much pride to serve these wonderful friends all these years, and it is our wish to continue doing so.

Sincerely,
Sam, Dora and Joe

Auntie's "story" about Sam's

Can you guess the time?

1. When was the first hot dog created? _____

2. When was the paper clip invented? _____

3. When was the first chocolate chip cookie made? _____

4. When was the umbrella invented? _____

5. What year was the monopoly game introduced? _____

6. When was the first tweet sent? _____

7. When did the internet begin? _____

8. When was the toothbrush invented? _____

9. When did the first McDonald's open? _____

10. When and who took the first selfie? _____

11. When was soap first used? _____

12. When was toilet paper first used? _____

13. What year did scotch tape appear? _____

14. When were disposable diapers invented? _____

15. When was the first swivel chair used? _____

16. When were shoes first made for left and right feet? _____

Answers

1. The first hot dogs as we know them today came from Germany. "Frankfurter" is claimed by Frankfurt in the 13th century. "Weiner" is claimed by Vienna (whose German name is Wien) in the 18th century. It wasn't until the 1860s that hot dogs/frankfurters/wieners were first sold in New York City pushcarts by German immigrants. The first Coney Island hot dog stand was opened in 1871.

2. Although there were many similar devices, William D. Middlebrook of Waterbury, CT. is credited with the first patent on the paper clip 1899. He later sold the patent to manufacturers Cushman and Denison who called it the "Gem."

3. The first chocolate chip cookie was made by Ruth Graves Wakefield in 1937 who ran the Toll House Restaurant in Massachusetts with her husband. She called it "The toll House Crunch Cookie."

4. The first recorded use of the umbrella or sun-protecting parasol was in ancient Egypt, over 3500 years ago.

5. The first version of Monopoly was known as The Landlord's Game, designed by American Elizabeth Magie and patented in 1904. By 1933 it was adapted into the game we know today.

6. It was originally called "TWTR" and referred to 140-character message that was set up in 2006. Jack Dorsey wrote "just setting up my twttr."

7. The first internet message was sent over a US Department of Defense project called the ARPANET (Advanced Research Projects Agency) in 1969, from computer science Professor Leonard Kleinrock's Laboratory at the University of California to the Stanford Research Institute.

8. The toothbrush, as we know it today, was invented in 1938. However, early forms have existed since 3000 BC

9. The original McDonald's was opened in 1940 by brothers Richard and Maurice McDonald (Dock and Mac). It was located in San Bernardino, CA - a drive-in with car hop service. In 1955 Ray Kroc founded McDonald's Systems, Inc. and bought the rights to the McDonald's name. McDonald's sold its 100 millionth hamburger by 1958.

10. Although the selfie has a long history in self-portraits, the first photo selfie was taken in 1939 by Robert Cornelius. He set up his camera and ran into the frame (there were no remotes).

11. Babylonian clay containers dated 2800 B.C. had inscriptions for the earliest written soap recipes.

12. People used any available stuff to clean themselves after "going to the bathroom" – from leaves, grass, sticks, clay pieces, and anything handy. It

13. wasn't until the 6th century in medieval China that sheets of paper were used. In 1891 Seth Wheeler patented his invention of toilet paper on a roll.

14. Engineer and banjo-player Richard Drew invented the first transparent adhesive tape – scotch tape – in 1930.

15. Marion Donovan, a Post WWII mother and housewife, introduced disposable diapers in 1949 and patented them in 1951.

16. Thomas Jefferson invented the first swivel chair in 1776 and used it to write much of *The Declaration of Independence.*

17. William Young, a Philadelphia Boot Maker first made shoes specifically for left and right feet in 1800. However, it wasn't generally accepted until the American Civil War.

Thank you for reading these timepieces!

Remember your own timepieces and share them with your friends and family.

Read more cutting-edge Book Web Minis

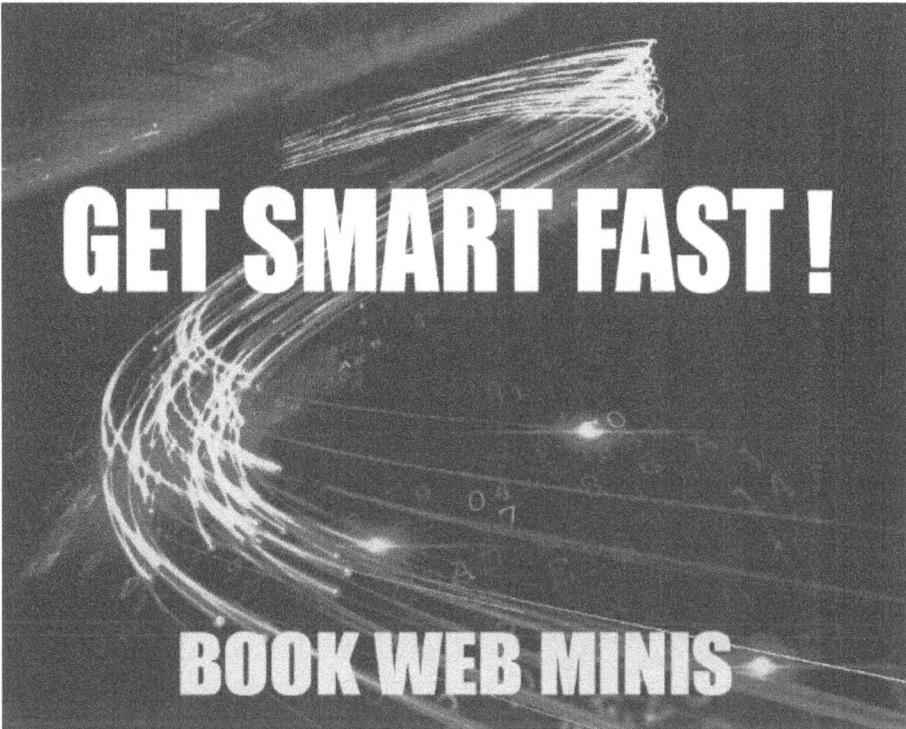

Book Web Minis are fun, fast, and hot. Mini books (50-70 pages long) explore up-to-the-minute facts, photos, content, and quizzes to make you the pro. Share with friends, family, and colleagues. Don't wait – get them from Amazon.com.

Bestselling Titles:

Paranormal Is My Normal
SOARING!
Selfies: Picture Perfect
PocketCash: Your Way
Photo Power: Hidden Stories

Check out Book Web Fiction

Amazon #1 Bestsellers!

Page turners bursting with Haunted family trees, strange lovers, photo insights, and psychopaths burst into life. Broken Books reinvent the thriller, blending fact, fiction, and photos into riveting unforgettable stories **Go to amazon.com** to purchase these bestsellers in ebook, print (black & white), and collector's edition (full color print).

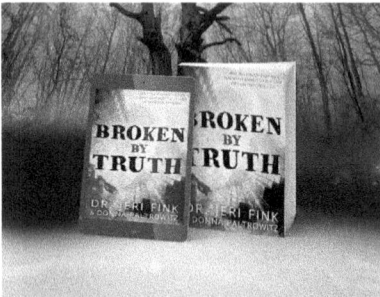

Mack aimed the white gun at the stage. The shot blasted through the studio, reverberating off lights, cameras, and booms. For an endless moment no one moved. A red hole appeared on her forehead. Her eyes widened in confusion as blood spattered her cream-colored Armani suit. *Book 1*

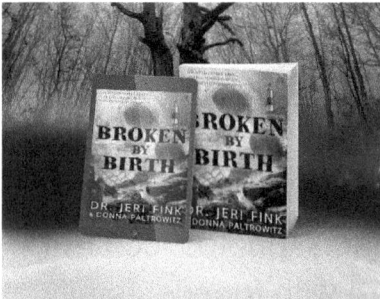

Joshua enters the world in a gritty basement apartment beneath the shadow of an old water tower. He was beaten, neglected, and by the end of his first day of life, abandoned. Joshua's bone-chilling story is followed from the womb through foster care, and into the terror of his forever home. *Book 2*

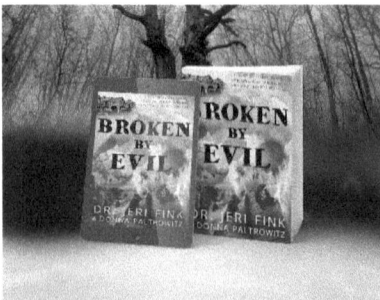

Everyone is terrified of Joshua. Drowned cats, dissected squirrels, and burning dogs are his playthings. No one knows what the child thinks or will do next. The Senator, Aldi and Cal, Sage, and Grandma Espie, among others, return in this blood-curdling thriller. *Book 3*

Read riveting Book Web's Historical Fiction

Go back in time to discover how evil thrived in the past. Meet the ancestors of the characters in the first three Broken Books and follow their haunted family trees. Available in print and ebook on amazon.com

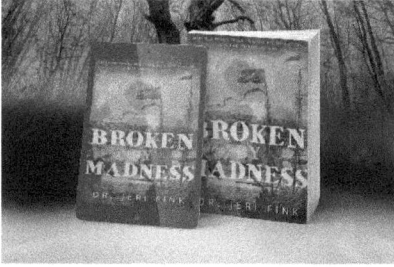

A small group of refugees settle in 1654 New Amsterdam's *Jews Alley* - against Director-General Peter Stuyvesant's objections. A psychopath emerges, stalking the Alley, leaving his bloody calling card at their doorstep. What happens when the psychopath evolves? *Book 4*

Hannah and Esperanza flee The Inquisition, joining expelled Spanish Jews in 1492. They find refuge on a tiny Portuguese farm with two old Christian peasants. A traveler turns the sisters into the royal soldiers. Simao, a psychopathic soldier and his band arrive on the farm and scar the sisters for generations to come. *Book 5*

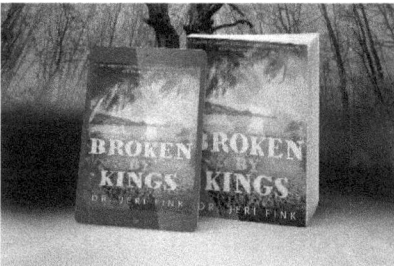

Esperanza is kidnapped by the King's soldiers. She joins 2000 Jewish children shipped to the malaria-infested African island of Sao Tome. The Portuguese soldiers take children as their sex slaves. Many are seized by the newly arrived psychopathic soldier, Simao. Can they escape the evil of kings? *Book 6*

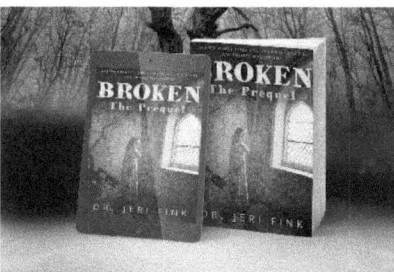

The Broken Saga begins in 1492. The Tapiadors are Conversos (Secret Jews) betrayed to The Inquisition. Armed soldiers arrest them. The two sisters escape through a hidden tunnel while soldiers drag their parents to the torture chambers. *Book 7*

Links

Dr. Jeri Fink: www.jerifink.com

Bookweb Minis: www.bookwebminis.com

Bookweb Fiction: www.hauntedfamilytrees.com

Photo Insights (original "feel-good" photos delivered weekly, for free, into your email box):

http://hauntedfamilytrees.com/landing-page

Timepieces

www.ingramcontent.com/pod-product-compliance
Lightning Source LLC
Chambersburg PA
CBHW081222020426
42331CB00012B/3077

9781941882290